Primer on the Hereafter

Primer on the Hereafter

Poems by Steve McOrmond

Wolsak and Wynn

Cover image: "Willowcrows," Acryllic on 23K gold leaf
© Suezan Aikins, www.suezanaikins.com
Cover design: Silas White
Author's photograph: Janet Hoops
Typeset in Garamond
Printed by The Coach House Printing Company, Toronto, Ontario

Some of these poems first appeared in *Arc*, *Breathing Fire 2: Canada's New Poets* (Nightwood, 2004), *Event*, *The Fiddlehead*, *Geist*, *Grain*, *Greenboathouse.com*, *Jacket* (Australia), *The New Quarterly*, *nthposition.com* (UK), *The Malahat Review*, *Maisonneuve.org*, *Prairie Fire*, *PRISM International*, *Eyewear* (UK) and *Qwerty*. The author thanks the editors of these publications.

The publishers gratefully acknowledge the support of the Canada Council for the Arts, the Ontario Arts Council, and the Book Publishing Industry Development Program (BPIDP) for their financial assistance.

The Canada Council of the Arts, the Ontario Arts Council, and the Toronto Arts Council provided financial support to the author during the completion of this book.

Wolsak and Wynn Publishers Ltd.
Suite #102, 69 Hughson Street North
Hamilton, Ontario
L8R 1G5
www.wolsakandwynn.ca

Library and Archives Canada Cataloguing in Publication

McOrmond, Steven Craig, 1971-
        Primer on the hereafter / Steve McOrmond

Poems.
ISBN 1-89487-12-8

TITLE.

PS8575.O74P75 2006   C811'.54   C2006-904274-8

For my parents,

Edward and Mina McOrmond

Contents

I

Crows   13
Self-portrait as the middle-aged fool   14
Come play on my island   15
Yankee gale, 1851   16
Winter songs   18
Man in a room full of nudes   20
Dandelions   21
The lobster   22
Searletown, R.R.2   24
Communion   25
Norman   27
Lolly   29
White Mazda blues   32
Scales Pond   34
Leonid showers   36
Crows (reprise)   37
So this is goodbye   38

II

Meander & Co.   41
The second coming   42
Popular science   43
Flittermouse   44
With apologies to the Far East Fortune Cookie Company   45
Stockholm   46
Dear reader   47
Happy hour   48
Armchair   49
Toronto life   50
The linear model   51
Bad dialogue   52

III

53E Express   55
Dog day afternoon   56
Rabbit ears   58
The little girl in *Poltergeist*   59
Luminous veil   60
Haulage   61
Self-portrait #33   62
Heat, smog, ultraviolet   63
Primer on the hereafter   64
What remains   66
Blue jay   67
Clear-cut, as seen from above   69
Close encounter   71
Ötzi   73
Whitefish Lake   75
Red planet   80
Rabbit ears (2)   81
Basilica   82
Keith Jarrett: The Köln Concert   84
Finch Station   85

Notes on the poems   86
Acknowledgements   88

For all you I
Have neglected, ignored,
Left to stew in your own juices,
Not been that friend that is approaching,
I ask forgiveness, a song new like rain.
Please sing it to me.

— John Ashbery, "Posture of Unease"

I

We drive until we can't remember
where we're from.

– Eric Hill, "Last Orphan Wine"

Crows

They congregate, clotted darkness
in the old birches behind the house.

The conscience of this sleepy town,
our sins cloud the air and stick to them.

A few blocks south on Dorchester Street,
the locals are blowing their pogey cheques

on vodka and rye. The party's already old
when we get home from work and night-blooming

jasmine fills the room with the scent of tea.
Before this day is through, someone will break

a bottle on the edge of the table, another will go
to hospital with a bad case of Van Gogh's ear.

A woman will lock herself in the bathroom and pray
her lover passes out before kicking down the door.

In the morning, crows will wake us
from a tangle of uneasy dreams.

Boisterous in the treetops, tuneless
as 10,000 cigarettes, they're singing our song.

Self-portrait as the middle-aged fool

You've come a long way
past quotidian drunkenness, past caring
whether you left the stove on, the whereabouts
of your father's deer rifle, loaded
with one in the chamber. No reason to hurry home
now that everyone but the dog has gone, and yet
where else would you go? Past last call,
throwing up in the back of the cab, and later
the dry heaves, you arrive at this clarity
like lucid dreaming. You have reached a place
where Heidegger makes sense, and stumbling
across the lawn, you can smell it: first snow,
not the end, but how an ending
is supposed to feel. In the yard, the maples
have made their arrangements, scattering
sepia photographs of themselves
on the sidewalk, and the only
suitable gesture is to weep.

Come play on my island

I can't blame you
for claiming this place as your own
personal theme park.
                            For you,
there is only summer. Every curve
in the road brings a new photograph –
red cliffs climbing out of the sea, field upon field
of white blossoms, a wharf where boats
christened *The Maggie-Mae* and *Aurora Dawn*
depart for the fishing grounds.
                            How authentic:
the old salt at the helm and the boy
untying the bow line. You might pause
a minute and imagine everything you see
transformed – a winter gale blowing
off the gulf for days, cabin fever, accidents
involving teenagers, icy roads, alcohol.
The bare bones of living here – then return
to applying sun screen and minding the kids
don't drown as the tide comes in.

The fine art of self-deprecation:
I laugh along when you feel obliged
to affect a bad Maritime accent
or complain about the loaded hay wagon
leading a mile-long procession into town. I wait
tables for five bucks an hour and smile
as you like it:
                            Here, let me
fasten this plastic bib around your neck
while the cook in the kitchen
drops the lobster, still living, into boiling water.

Yankee gale, 1851

After the storm, time to rebuild
the windmill, butcher the cow
struck by lightning, and salvage
what we may from loss.

Tomorrow we will row out
to the ghost ship riding at anchor
in the looking-glass: sails torn, deck
swept bare. Crew, doubtless, dead.

Advertised for sale in *Hazard's Gazette*:
the ill-fated *Franklin Dexter*. Five persons
picked from her sides, perfectly naked,
flesh coming away in our fingers.

The schooner *Shipjack* waterlogged
near Rustico: *We have taken off*
ten dead and 30 barrels of mackerel.
Westward of Cove Head, a nameless

brig gone to pieces with all hands:
I have recovered a quantity of empty
Puerto Rico sugar hogsheads, which I mean
to put to use in the making of spirits.

Will the drink be potent enough to forget
the body of a man pulled from the surf
with a boy lashed to his back?
We've lost track of the souls put to rest

this week on Hog Island; men stooped over
from digging graves. How does one begin
the letter informing a New Englander
four sons and a nephew are drowned?

More than a hundred vessels in all
wrecked or stranded in the saddle
of the north shore, and we left to reap
a terrible harvest. To be sold Friday next.

Winter songs

– Gilles Vigneault

1.

For the crows, austerity's
angels, acid-etched on the whiteness.

For in the dark of the cold cellar, the jelly jars
switch on, begin to pulse.

For your ears are burning
with frostbite; somewhere the dead
are discussing your works and deeds.

2.

For the man who abandons his car
in a snowdrift on the county line road
must not presume he'll return

next morning, the Buick
shagged with ice, a woolly
mastodon waiting to be exhumed.

For the land shivers
in a bone-white corset, string of icy pearls,
and she is calling, calling

across the fields, the snow
deep and trackless, lit
by a moon called hunger.

3.

For the youngest, who had to crawl
out the kitchen window, both doors
blocked, shovel the way back in.

For this too is recorded in the ledger,
its cover black as feathers.

Man in a room full of nudes

(Beaverbrook Art Gallery, Fredericton, N.B.)

This wing of the gallery has been reserved
for a reception, rows of stacking chairs,
a slim podium from which, this evening,
the artist will say a few words. Behind the lectern,
a wall of nudes in various positions of repose.
All seats vacant except for one: an old man
staring at the panoply of female forms.
So many lovely breasts, painted in oils,
some shaped like pears, others cantaloupes,
and who would blame him if he leaned in
close to the canvas to sniff their ripeness.
Having intruded, should I clear my throat?
But his thoughts are years away, perhaps trysting
with the coy maid in the gilt-framed, archetypal garden.
Her body has just begun to bloom, and her eyes
suggest there are many shady places
we might lie down; as if all pretty flowers
long to be picked. The man might recently
have lost his wife, or maybe a daughter, the first time
in his life there hasn't been a woman around the house.
There hangs about him the loneliness of food courts.
Though limbs fail, and the mind surrenders
to incertitude, bewilderment, the longing
never leaves – Goethe, at age 72, falling in love
with a 19-year-old, Ulrike, from the spa town
in the mountains, how he must have lain awake,
thinking over and over, no good will come of this,
none. The year I worked nights in the nursing home.
Making my rounds, I'd find the old men snoring, ghostly
erections lifting the thin white sheets. The body, pale
and heavy in sleep, resigned to its decrepitude,
but desire still wide-eyed, hungry,
hoisting its tiny sail.

Dandelions

You'd think they'd have learned
to frown on fortune, a rich history
of beheadings, generations fallen
beneath spinning blades. Perennial
war is all they know, bitter milk
runs through them, suffering
and exaltation. With the blissed-out
calm of kamikazes, they smile
at the push mower's headlong
advance, sink their teeth
deeper into the ground. Altogether
they make something bigger
than one alone: a sea of swaying
mantras, they raise their bright
faces to the sun. The two-stroke
engine marches to a different tune, loves
the smell of mixed gas in the morning.
It chews up their fierce quiet
and spits it out. The satisfaction
of a job well done, the Lawn-Boy dozes
in the back of the shed, surrounded
by the oily glimmer of tools.
But the seeds are sewn. Soon enough
an army of snowy-haired monks
will take the field, sage white heads
awaiting wind.

The lobster

The new assistant cook, whose job it is to chaperone the lobster on its short journey from tank to pot, is having second thoughts. The chef, a jovial and pompous man, assures him that, since they do not have vocal chords, they cannot scream. The sound he hears coming from the stock pot is air whistling from the body cavity as it expands. Still, he can feel them quake in his hands, mild vibrations like the buzzing of a honeybee. His heart, if it could, would make of itself something hard: a claw.

He has been reading up. A lobster with one claw is called a cull; with no claws, a pistol. Size matters. Females find an enormous crusher claw irresistible. If torn off in a fight or accident, the missing appendage will grow back slowly. We lack this regenerative capacity. His uncle who lost a hand in the mill – not a day goes by he doesn't feel that phantom itch.

The doldrums between late lunch and early supper. The chef busies himself with marinades. One of the waitresses nods on her way to grab a smoke near the grease trap. At the end of a shift, the spatters congealed on the floor by the fryer can be rolled up like a carpet. He thumbs through what's left of yesterday's classifieds. If there's an easier way to make minimum wage, it isn't listed.

What he envies most is the lobster's ability to moult. He is tired of wearing the same thin skin day in, day out. In an escape worthy of Houdini, the lobster swallows water until its carapace lifts up and away from the tail and the membrane explodes. The body is shed first, then the head, the lining of the gills. Next the eyes pop out. It pulls and pulls, struggling to free meaty claws from their armour. *Voilà!* At last, the manacles fall away.

The bell again. Someone has made her selection from the glass tank out front. Time to play pallbearer in his white apron and hairnet. May the woman's toes swell up with gout, may she choke on the coral. Rolling up his sleeve, he thinks of Sartre's recurring fear: a lobster scuttling across the bottom of his dreams, sculling itself backwards, propelled by its powerful tail. O samurai, O queerling, O grasshopper of the deep.

Searletown, R.R.2

I choose dusk to say goodbye. The grey barn
out back and the chicken coop, still falling down
after fifteen years. How my father
tried and failed to live as a gentleman farmer.
The hens stopped laying, the rooster died.
No heat in the upstairs bedrooms after the pipes froze
and he shut off the plumbing. Mornings
you could see your breath up there. In less than a month,
I'll pack my things and move away for good.
East of the barn, the apple orchard where I made out
with the Noonan twins. Beyond that,
the sandy lane leading back to the woods.
Patches of snow in June holed up under the spruces,
fugitive. I hid out there too, most days after school.
Now I make my way through the pasture, fermenting
cow patties, bluebottles flaunting their fat, oily
iridescence. Stumble through waist-high thistles, elastic
spruce limbs, down to the banks of the Bradshaw River.
Trout flicker in the shallows. The warm weather
will have muddied their flesh. On the slope,
nature is reclaiming the junk pile. Toadstools spill
from a bottomless milking pail, yellow-jackets nest
beneath a blown radiator. Deeper, you'd find broken china,
horse bones. Here mosquitoes hatch in the millions, rising
in dense clouds. I squat, wanting to commit even the bug bites
to memory. Soon foxes will nose along in the dark,
the screech owl will glide over the fields, a swath of silence.
When this place no longer knows me.

Communion

At recess, we assemble by the electric fence
bordering the Johnstone's cow pasture – Bloyce,

wearing filth from the farm like a second skin,
the Matheson boys, whose father drowned

that summer on an oil rig. And Michael,
the lawyer's son, his singular ambition to serve

on the Supreme Court. We all join hands
and for those fifteen minutes before the bell rings,

we are one body, no longer separated
into rich kids and poor kids, bullies and victims.

The current travels through us, a centipede's
hundred legs crawling up one arm, across the chest,

down the other arm. Our bones itch, we taste
metal. Each of us must take a turn – the last boy

in the chain, a marionette, eyes glassy with panic,
struggling to let go but gripped by a passion

that takes his grin and shakes, a tongueless
scream that can overwhelm the heart. For Michael – no,

for us all – a dress rehearsal. By the end of semester,
he'd complain of a stiff neck and fever.

Meningitis. His body interred in a zinc-lined casket
by order of the health department. Mike, maybe you

could help me: I see his face, but what was the name
of the boy who started it all, our conductor,

who first took a deep breath, reached out
and made a fist around the wire.

Norman

The only guy in grade nine who can grow
a moustache, you've got the balls to go toe-to-toe

with Father Tate – cracking your knuckles in class,
hawking up a gob and spitting on his shoe.

Your casual relationship with violence,
a dreadful economy. You know precisely how

to inflict the most damage with the least expenditure,
making an example of someone twice your size,

forcing him to turtle on the ground.
Once you kicked me so hard in the ass, I spent

my lunch hour locked in the toilet and the teacher
sent me home. Still, without your help, I'll never

pass algebra. Your mind cinches tight
as a rabbit snare on integers and equations. You might

make a mathematician someday if anyone mentions
it's feasible to dream beyond the family farm – rotten

shingles on house and barn, dog barking on a chain,
nowhere to hide from the heat. Invited after school

to keep you company in the cab of the tractor,
how readily I accept you as my mentor

in the fine art of intimidation and fear. My chicken neck
and Coke-bottle glasses, you must recognize

the perfect apprentice. And maybe you're right –
I say nothing when you hoist the sick sow

onto your shoulder, heave it into the manure spreader.
I stand there on the John Deere, gripping the seat,

as you work the raw sludge of its scream
into the exhausted red field.

Lolly

(Mr. Wier's account, Wallace, Nova Scotia, March, 1855)

My dear wife, I am now convalescing
in the home of Mr. Hiram Gore,
a pig farmer of some repute.
His son William has been so kind
as to take down my thoughts.

There was nothing out of the ordinary
when we set out that morning –
Haszard and Smith returning
from studies in Philadelphia,
myself, the four-man crew.
I paid double fare for the luxury
of not having to get out and push.
The others eyeballing me, calculating
my weight as they would any trunk
or mail bag they'll have to hump
nine miles across the strait.

The weather was clear and fair
and we made good time
despite pressure ridges near to shore
where the ice hits bottom
and gangs up on itself, jagged peaks
with boulder fields and gullies in between.
We were half a mile from the island side
when it started to puff up. Then it began
to snow and the cliffs disappeared.

We kept on until we hit the lolly.
When salt water can't decide
whether to stay liquid or freeze, it turns
thick and dark as your black current jelly.

Too solid to pull an oar through, too
soft to walk on unless you're God's Son.
The men cursed and drew the boat up
onto the ice, turned it on its gunwales
and we huddled underneath. Two days
and nights like this, listening to snow
rasp against the wooden hull and the wind
which sounded like a cat being flayed.

Mr. Haszard had a little spaniel.
On the morning of the third day,
I held it down and Smith
slit its throat with my bone-handled knife.
We drank its blood, consumed
the flesh before it could freeze.
This we'd have done sooner,
but Haszard loved that dog.
"Loyalty and devotion,"
he muttered, his teeth chattering
from the cold. "Only animals
have never let me down
in these qualities." He wouldn't
touch the meat and I believe
he might have offered us
his own throat instead.

He wasn't the same after that.
We continued to drift, always
southeast toward the mainland.
On the fourth day, Mr. Haszard
grew delirious and could no longer
keep his feet. Sometime after dark,

he left us. When Smith woke,
he pulled off his heavy mitts
to close his friend's eyes.

We made shore the next morning,
a Tuesday. And yet it was too early
for rejoicing – the nearest farmhouse
a two-mile walk through deep snow.
Neither Smith nor I could go on,
so the others left us, saying they'd soon
return with blankets and soup.

The rest is not an easy thing
for a man to tell his wife.
I have lost both feet above the ankles
and all my fingers that could tie a trout fly,
play the fiddle, unlace your bodice.
I'm an old man, but I had hoped
to have more use for them.

Still, I suppose I should feel lucky.
The physician says I may
come through this. I should like to
get home to you, but I fear
the worst. When I close my eyes,
I fall overboard into a blackness
that congeals around my limbs.
It will not let me surface.
It will not let me sink.

White Mazda blues

Leave the old man dozing in front of the TV,
three fingers of bourbon in a coffee mug.

Jay's in the driveway, gunning the engine.
Pulling onto the pavement, he squeals bald tires,

I flip my house the bird, lights wavering
in the rear-view, just the way I like it.

We'll spend all night hurtling over bad roads
with no place to go. Three thousand car parts

flying in loose formation, oil pan swathed in duct tape,
floor on the passenger side like soggy cardboard.

When my seat drops through, travelling 60 mph,
Jay jams a snowbrush underneath to prop the post up.

At a certain age, this is all the freedom there is,
a gutless four-banger, would-be boudoir on wheels.

Jay swears he doesn't know much, but he's damned
sure you're not a man unless you can drive stick.

He says we're the sons of drunkards, ourselves
drunkards in the making, and as long as we stay

that's all we'll ever be. If this road has a name
I never learned it, though I could

navigate its hairpins and straightaways
with my eyes closed. Gears are simple, easy

to believe you're getting somewhere, clutch,
downshift, punch the pedal. We'll ride

this shitbox straight to the wreckers or out west,
whichever comes first, and no one will catch us.

So much body-fill, we'd appear on radar
as a low-flying flock of starlings.

Scales Pond

You're supposed to be sleeping over
at Jane's but you're with your freckled boy.

In a booth at the back of the diner,
he carves a heart with your initials

deep in the pine. His penknife flicks love.
He blows the shavings off the table, asks

if you want to go for a ride – and you do.
No matter his idea of romance is a six-pack

under your feet, the Freetown Road
unravelling like a run-on sentence.

You hold the wheel, he leans way out,
tries to peg fence posts with the empties.

When he takes the cut-off without asking,
you can guess what's on his mind, desire

a dangling participle. No matter his breath
tastes like beer and cigarettes. No matter

the way he shoves his fingers up there,
like you're a puppet he can manipulate

from the inside out. He kills the lights,
the world comes slowly

back into focus. Empty parking lot, the dam
where your brothers fish, his hand on your knee.

You stare out the windshield – dark clouds,
not even a sliver of moon

to cut the pond's slack and give you
no good reason.

Leonid showers

Far from the city lights, the sky is roaring.
Particles no bigger than grains of sand

strike the atmosphere at 40 miles a second.
Some gutter fast as they fall, others

shoot over the horizon, just grazing
earth's envelope, a lion flicking its tail.

I don't know how long we stood
by the side of the road, trying to fit the ellipses

of our lives into something grander, mean
solar time, debris clouds, celestial

precipitation. The century is ending;
by New Year's you and I will be through.

We stayed until our necks
ached from looking up

until we had nothing
left to wish for.

Crows (reprise)

They roost, ridiculous and sublime
in the old birch trees behind the house.

They've had a long day: mobbing the neighbour's
orange tabby crawling on her belly

through the long grass, eating the ass
out of a road-killed skunk, haute cuisine.

The teenager whose bedroom window
faces onto the backyard and the birches

isn't here now as dusk settles like volcanic ash.
It'll be after midnight when he stumbles home

drunk on a school night, four tries before his key
fits in the door. Early next morning, crows

will wake him from a fitful sleep. He'll consider
buying a pellet gun from Canadian Tire.

Loitering in the treetops, they are
every dumb mistake he's ever made.

So many it's a wonder the branches hold them.

So this is goodbye

The story of the Island is the story of paradise:
we have always had to leave.

In the morning it'll be your turn – your mother
standing in the driveway in her pink housecoat,

father seeing you off, firm handshake, stiff hug.
You won't permit yourself a single tear, not

when all you've ever wanted is to get away.
This sandbar lodged in the gulf like a lump

in the throat. Small world, and getting smaller
at the mercy of ice ride-up, storm surge.

Like the beaches of our youth, grain by grain,
we are washed away, deposited elsewhere.

You'd need a tractor trailer for everything
you've forgotten, abandoned, taken for granted.

Intangibles you never thought you'd miss
and miss already: the smell of the sea, salt

spiking the air, the cacophony of crows.
Tomorrow when you go, all your worldly

possessions will ride with you in the back
of the U-Haul: Goodwill furniture, a dead uncle's

colour TV, several tons of books packed too heavily
in liquor boxes, and wedged behind the wheel well,

a finicky six-foot tall Ficus benjamina
you hope won't lose all its leaves.

II

The sun shone, having no alternative,
on the nothing new.

– Samuel Beckett

Meander & Co.

I just hope we get lost and soon.
The road has funnelled down to a rabbit run.
Wilderness wraps around us, sticky.
The compass needle spins and spins.

We passed the last signpost ages ago.
Moving deeper into rain, its wordless persistence.
Murky underwater light.
The spruce trees shuddering like wet dogs.

No one will find us.
This isn't your permanent record.
It's a long day's hike into the gathering dark.
Are we home yet and do you want to?

The second coming

There's been some mistake and now
a crowd is gathering – honestly, you
don't deserve the keys to the city, roses
and women's underwear falling at your feet.

You're a bad haircut waiting for a bus.
You're a short order
cook at a greasy spoon, another stained shirt
hurrying to make the night shift.

You're anyone, the sum of memory:
father was a ruined pillar. Mother,
slender vine, inseparable and lonely.
Go jump in the lake – and you did.

You're a faded pair of Levi's, knees
winking at the cameras. You're the future,
neither bright nor certain. The song replaying
in your head doesn't even know its name.

Popular science

You never tire of looking at the stars.
Who wouldn't want to be so bright and distant?
Lately you perceive a static in your brain
like that prickly feeling in your extremities
as your limbs recover from having fallen asleep.
A long time ago, you believed it might be possible
to find one key that would unlock the whole shebang —
those giddy days teaching amusement park physics.
You know now there are more keys than stars, and many more
locks than keys. The answer is here though it's nothing
we can decipher between breakfast and dinner. It's not easy
to keep the mind limber and alert when the only chores left
are a few trips to the green grocer, sniffing out the ripest cantaloupe;
or to accept some small consolation: maybe it isn't so bad
for us to go on mostly puzzled by the clouds.

Flittermouse

High frequency peeps and pops,
telemetry from the twilight zone,
and a soft *thwup, thwup, thwup*,
part pterodactyl, part Bela
Lugosi in a playful mood,
snapping a wet dishtowel.

This moon-skittering gothic
beastie sounds down starless, shoots
tangled boughs of the old apple, skims
mosquito clouds, liquid
warmth in gulps.
                              Whirring
blades, serrated, sharp
click of teeth low overhead –
food processor with wings,

                                        bug-eyed.
You can't steer this dream:
loose where it hinges,
wingbones and jaws wide,
flying off from no centre –
sway-skinned, millennial,

swift.

With apologies to the Far East Fortune Cookie Company

Good news will come to you by mail.
You will inherit some money or a small piece of land.
Your business will assume vast proportions.
Listen not to vain words of flapping gums.
Your success in life must be earned with earnest efforts.
He who hurries cannot walk with dignity.
Keep your plans secret for now.
Birds are entangled by their feet, men by their tongues.
It is better to have a hen tomorrow than an egg today.
Sing and rejoice, fortune is smiling on you.
Hand that touch this slip have no more worries.
Now is the time to finish up old tasks.
There is a prospect of a thrilling journey at hand.
You may attend a party where strange customs prevail.

Stockholm
(for Matthew & Charmaine Tierney)

To dwell between the snowy fastness
and the ice-locked sea, in a city of blondes.

One must have heard the existential scream,
hands over ears, the huge Os of mouth and eyes.

Know it can begin with nothing more extreme
than the flat's creaky floors, the old radiator ticking.

A fragile ecosystem: the furless, burrowing heart
and the Allen key of the mind.

Eventually, one might acquire a taste for hardcore
pornography and cod roe paste in squeeze tubes.

Held hostage in the bank vault of winter,
the captive will identify with the captor.

However peacefully it seems to fall,
there is suppressed violence in the snow.

Dear reader

We have so little in common.
I have never owned a dry goods store
in Wyoming, nor picked mushrooms
in the dark forest outside St. Petersburg.
At a dinner party, we'd have nothing to say.
Red or white? Pass the yams.
Then how can I reach you, or you me? Perhaps
we can agree to meet each other halfway,
warily, as on a stone bridge at midnight.
Cordon of fog, sound of running water
far beneath. The air dank, the stones,
saturated with symbolism, green and slick
as fish scales. A place where prisoners have been
exchanged, and jilted lovers have leapt, futureless,
into the void. Bring terms and conditions, I will come
prepared to answer for my laziness, my lack of talent.
I never meant to disappoint you, every word I sent
whispering across the irreconcilable distances
was signed *Que Besu Su Mano*, Who Kisses Your Hand.

Happy hour

You've fallen in love with an old
friend's wife. You keep meeting her
in dreams, she wafts a dusky scent
across the table, sets you adrift in her eyes.
You can talk about nothing for hours.
A second-story man, you're used to taking
whatever catches your fancy. Always
the quiet one in school, dear old aunties
pegged you for a priest, but you knew
your studied unobtrusiveness would pay off
bigger. On hands and knees, you're a shoo-in
for front hall tables at midnight. Homeowners
throw coats on top of you, proceed to the bedroom.
You wear the lady's sable and slip out
French doors. Or so you tell me over doubles,
neat. I have that kind of face: strangers
approach and uncork themselves.

Armchair

My daddy warned me about
boys like you, no good
drifter, a little shopworn
in crushed felt and a faint
moist odour of mushrooms.

You're just another pickpocket
after petty change, a girl
draped across your arm.
You and me, baby, we're something
shady waiting to happen.

Because you rub me the right way.
Because I dig your easy springs.
Because my daddy told me…
I pick you up
on the corner and drag you home.

Alone together in the elevator,
now coy, now flannel-mouthed,
now. Into your threadbare arms
where all the appetites
slouch down and sleep.

Toronto life

But my, when Vera was young
and a leg model in post-war London – white gloves
and other strenuous niceties – she cut quite a swath.
Husbands weren't used to that sort of thing: sex on the table,
sex wound tightly around the neck, the full treatment.
The day after, these gentlemen, forced to debate
policies and beliefs, were speechless.
"We are severely constrained by the Official Plan."

Freedman was different, distinguished
himself by being poorer and crazier than the rest.
The family coat of arms no substitute for satchels of money.
"To do this, we need to act now." Everything so overcharged!
He shook up the architecture. "Now listen, my dear,
next we're buying a restaurant, a ravine, the southern slope."

But Vera had a head on her wonderful ticket: He's a big liar,
she thought. There was prodigious evidence even then
his career ambitions would come to a rather gentle
nothing. Forced to sell the place in the country,
put the chandelier in storage. They lived in rented digs
thereafter, Freedman suing associates for fees.

Now the boys are grown, postcards from brothels
and correctional facilities, Vera feels that familiar itch.
High time these storied legs took a walk.
Yet there are new limits on her ruthlessness.
Freedman wastes in an overstuffed chair, needs help
opening the gin bottles. He's had a run in. Vera remains.

The linear model

Your last nightfall in the Great Basin,
where gamblers skin out and whiten
like clockwork. Where cold is lips
curled back and the wind is molars.
Where there's mercury, and greased dark
comes on like an express train from Reno.

Someone you scarcely know has tied you
down on the tracks, made sure the ropes
were not too tight, but tight enough. Now he's
gone and, strange, you're lonely for him.
Nobody ever tried to make you famous.
The train roars applause.

You're in the spotlight, the white
tunnel of its travelling. Engines and
their single-minded momentum. Night is
a vehicle of regret. Dazed cattle cars
and heavy machinery into the dry heart,
hurtling. Your long impatience over.

This is your life, the back page
of your local newspaper between ads
for furnaces and vacuums. Someone cuts out
a neat rectangle with its misspellings. All
you wanted, to be loved like this. He lays you down
in a drawer with stopped watches. Forever.

Bad dialogue

puts the pickle on the shit sandwich: *Hot,*
ain't it? Yes, hot. You wish he'd shut up
and shoot something – for dinner, preferably.
Stiff and car sore, spikes of Russian thistle
festering in your palm, you'd murder
the pharmacist for a bottle of codeine.

Sure, you could split, try to get your old job back
waitressing at the Nowhere Café. But you're a sucker
for a man with vision: he squints at the map, his dark eyes
tunnelling like moles all the way to Mexico where maybe
you can, like he says, make it as a dancer – no, this isn't
Hollywood in the thirties, black hats and white hats,

it's real life, gritty and tragic, shot on a shoestring.
Tomorrow, early, you'll drive into town,
Searchlight, Pahrump or Duckwater, there'll be
gunplay, hostages as usual, and this time, surely,
you'll come out the losers. A sad ending
for the whole misdirected mess. So why not

cut your losses and go? Your leading man's a psycho.
Worse, banal. You tell him so, concisely: *It's*
no good. I'm pissing off. Well, now you've done it,
gone and hurt his feelings. Slow as molasses, tears
gel on his cheeks and he's rooting in his pack for what?
A Kleenex? Jew's-harp? The Smith & Wesson? *Kaboom.*

III

I lived in one place. I want to die in another.

– Donald Revell, "The Northeast Corridor"

53E Express

Swallowed whole, the bus
is pushed slowly through
the morning rush, peristaltic
rhythm, stop-and-go. Old movies
where the actors sit in a parked car
pretending to drive while the scenery flickers
on a screen behind them, a moveable frieze.
Past Canadiana Drive, Storybook
Lane, and coming up on the left,
the gated community: groomed lawns
a shade of green not found in nature.
While we wait at the intersection,
dozens of buried sprinklers
stand at attention, geysers of
shimmering light, a renaissance
water park in France, before mobs
smash the walls, before the guillotine,
the sewers welling up with blood.
Pressed together like matches in a book,
we are getting tired of the same old story.
What keeps us from marching off
at the next stop to ignite revolution
will not keep us forever. As sure as our bodies
knock and jostle against one other, flutes
of nitroglycerin, we dream of slipping
through the trimmed hedge, over
the garden gate, making off
with all we can carry. Vincenzo Peruggia
strolling into the Louvre on a warm day
in August, 1911, heading straight
for the Mona Lisa, tucking her
beneath his coat and walking
out again, whistling a tune.

Dog day afternoon

It lacks *gravitas*. A pigeon has pecked a hole
through a slice of bread, now it bobbles

at my feet, wearing an Elizabethan collar
of stale whole-wheat. A delivery truck

lumbers past in low gear and the ground
jolts and whinges, no guarantee it won't

gape open underfoot. If this were my last day
on earth, I'd want to spend it

with the nightshift workers running errands,
dark circles around their eyes, young mothers

bending into strollers, people en route
to doctors' appointments, bracing themselves

for bad news. I would move through the city
like a camera, eavesdropping

on the conversations of teenagers who ditch
Poli-Sci to sit in coffee shops, observe

a moment of silence for those abandoned
bicycles chained to light poles, rusty frames,

bent rims, rotten tires. Archaeologists,
reading the ruins, pouring dust through a sieve,

will judge us by what we throw away,
how we lived in the foothills of the century.

Staring out the window of the bagel place,
through the cloudy sediment of car exhaust,

I watch a blind woman going slowly, surely
about her business, the slender white stick

dips and veers in front of her, a seismograph's
needle, barely touching the sidewalk.

Rabbit ears

We couldn't leave them there – the neighbours'
basement having disgorged its contents on the lawn

like a cat coughing up a hairball: cook books,
dehumidifier, unused strips of quarter-round.

Amid the debris, the Bakelite TV set and portable
antenna awaiting instructions from the mother ship.

Artifacts circa the age of Sputnik. "To the moon, Alice,
to the moon." Television's incunabula, how nostalgia

manifests itself in kitsch. A piece of masking tape
stuck to the dusty screen: "Works. $15." We haggle,

talk the old lady in the track suit down to ten.
Watching her sort the bills, osteoarthritis, liver spots,

I see a handsome woman in her early thirties
taking a break from housework, the baby

dozing in its crib, to watch a special report
coming to her live from the Dallas airfield.

She leans forward on the sofa's edge as JFK steps
down the gangway into a sea of outstretched hands.

The little girl in *Poltergeist*

While her parents sleep,
the television keeps her
under its watchful eye.
                    It figures
the dead would find a way
to speak through our most
ubiquitous device, its purpose
to interpret our desires, instruct us
in what we need.
                            Reaching
down from the ether, what would the dead
have to say? A sermon
full of tough love
I'd expect: same awful
program on every channel, voices
whispering inside the roar
of static.
                        The light
we walk into at the end of days, not
a white tunnel, diffuse and benign,
but the pixellated glare of TV
reading us head-to-toe
in a suddenly darkened room.

Luminous veil

*In 2002, the City of Toronto erected an elaborate suicide barrier along the
Bloor Street Viaduct which spans the Don Valley. Since the bridge opened
in 1918, over 480 people have leapt to their deaths below.*

Do you hope we'll slink home
and rethink our lives, find the god of

second chances? Maybe you'd prefer
we killed ourselves neatly, quietly,

in the seclusion of our own homes. We've tried
overwork, whiskey, fried food; they take too long.

10,000 steel rods, stainless, shimmering
in the morning light will only delay

the inevitable. Any rooftop or train tracks will do.
Think of us as your distant early warning, canaries

in the mineshaft. What is your life worth
and who pays? We mean our final gesture

to be no less political than those monks
who douse themselves in gasoline,

set their orange robes aflame. With our dumb
flesh and bones, the insignificant labour

of our bodies, which belong to us alone,
we wish to send you a message. Air mail.

Haulage

You could coast like this for years. Elevators carry you up to your spotless apartment and Glenn Gould playing Bach. Elevators drop you down to the parking garage and coolness of waiting automobiles – all that clearcoat shining in the semi-dark.

At times you feel like freight. Someone's lost the waybill, you're waiting to be delivered. Oh, there are drugs. A leather armchair that fits exactly the slouch of your spine. And there are the *Goldberg Variations*, succinct, austere, in the half-light. The hammer when it strikes the string is not in contact with anything touching the finger.

Most nights you manage. Sink into sleep and seldom remember your dreams. But tonight nothing works to take you up or down. Your precarious piece of the skyline is limbo. You think of John Cage emerging from a soundproof room to declare there is no such animal as silence. You think he was listening in the wrong place.

Cardiac flatline of tundra. A valley in the Antarctic where it hasn't rained in two million years. Or the island where you grew up. A stubble field at dusk, lying on your back watching a lone hawk hunt in the bruised haze. The piano articulating this distance at the heart of things – the way an atom is mostly empty space.

Radio silence. Far side of the moon.

Self-portrait #33

The figure leans over the bathroom sink,
his face blooms in the mirror, inspecting
a blemish or preparing to extract a grey hair.
The light does not love what it falls upon.

A man stitched together from pieces
of other men, blood memory, scraps.
Glassy eyes shoplifted from a taxidermist,
nose like the prow of a funeral ship.

Never one to look long or deeply, nor waste
time thinking about all those he has turned away.
One who would declare his present life sufficient
even as the hungry mob sets fire to his house.

Yet there is, seething beneath the calm surface,
a sadness that reminds one of an umbrella
discarded in the street; an unpronounced anger
which in time will cause the paint to blister.

Heat, smog, ultraviolet

Undeterred by the warnings, we move
along the street, pushing against a wall
of dead air. There's the homeless guy
on the corner, six white rats clinging to his coat sleeve.
His friend lifts a clenched fist to his ear: *Look, I'll call
you back on the landline.* This sends the rat man
into convulsions, his laughter a hemorrhage.
Either side of us, office towers stand watch
like paramilitary police in mirrored sunglasses.
We walk in their shadow, we who are
so much shadow and ruin. We glance upwards,
all that steel yawing in the wind, and our hearts, cheap
pocket watches, tick faster. This life we've built
can't bear its own weight.

Primer on the hereafter

Once you get past the wide-eyed amazement
of the freshly dead, you'll have to learn

to move shadowy limbs again, as one who has suffered
a stroke. Being incorporeal, you can't push off things:

sit down, you start to sink through the chair cushion,
then the floorboards, gravitating slowly

toward the basement. A gust of wind
can float you aloft, a stray balloon hovering

high above the street after the parade is over
and everyone gone home. The trick is to focus

on a place and time and think yourself there.
If you can't get the hang of it, don't worry.

You'll have all the time you need to practice.
Though you may move freely among the countries

of past and present, you will be a voyeur
peeping through a window. It isn't always happiness

to watch your life going on without you – spouses
remarry, children grow up, launching themselves

at the future like unguided missiles. You'll understand
why so many of the dead are couch potatoes, the glazed

eyes of junkies, drifting in and out of a vanished world:
cherished moments and grave mistakes repeated endlessly.

This you must know: it is expressly forbidden
to have commerce with those left behind. Keep trying

and you may be driven mad: one taps Morse code
on his lover's bed frame all through the night,

another attempts to write a letter, up to her wrists
in the guts of an old typewriter. All the words

she never had the chance to utter, transmogrified
into a heap of glass tears. The most you might do:

brush a picture crooked on its nail, persuade
the curtains to flutter. Things only the cat would notice.

What remains

Not the banged ear but tiny, delicate
bone works: hammer, anvil, stirrup.
Not the eyes but sockets,
not the tongue but teeth.
Not the heart.

Slug-soft, it
impales itself on razor wire,
grows wings, flutters
damp against stone
walls of the punishment cell,
Judas hole in the steel door
through which granular light
sifts.

The heart is a suicide, pages
torn from a notebook, perfect
columns of zeroes
tell us everything
we want to know.

Blue jay

This old world
still has a few tricks up its sleeve, today
it's a blue jay
perched on the eavestrough
of the building adjacent, smartass
heckler hurling jibes
from the nosebleeds – *Anyone here*
know the Heimlich
because this guy's choking.
                    You're right, Bird.
It's been awhile since I hammered one
over the fence. Your jeers irk me
from the blank screen, cup of coffee
gone cold on the desk, out
onto the balcony
in bathrobe and slippers. It appears
I'm a little underdressed, but
even in your blue ball gown, white
petticoat and black necklace,
you're no lady.
           I've watched
you descend on my parents' backyard
like a bad losing streak, scattering
the little brown jobs, muscling them out
of the feeder. Still, I covet
your broad vocabulary – soft nasal sounds,
gurgles and clicks. I've heard you
can mimic perfectly
the hiss of a red-tailed hawk.

                    Know something,
Bird? I've forgotten
how to put two words together
and make them sing. Please,
                    whisper
your raucous nothings in my ear, expound
upon philosophy and the Zen of Major League
Baseball. Caution me
never to be indulgent or neglectful, all things pass
quickly away. Last season's
home-run hitter can get bumped
to the bottom of the roster, end his career
riding pine in the dugout.
                    Without so much
as a good-bye note, you fly off
over the roofs
toward the lake and SkyDome,
a title in search of its poem.

Clear-cut, as seen from above

1.

Flying over slash,
skid trails, roads and flumes,
a creek greasy brown with runoff,
the little Dash-8 thrashed like a dog with an itch.
I thought about that column of too-thin air
reaching, *via negativa*, into the heavens.
File this image with the others, oil slick,
mushroom cloud, dead zone,
cross-reference with *Tokyo
was a wooden city*.

2.

How many rolls of double-ply
toilet tissue, disposable
plates for the office picnic, hardcovers
bound for the afterlife
of the remainder bin, how many
pencils, sheets of bond, sticky notes
upon which I jot my grocery lists,
appointments, the briefest of elegies – O
let my words signify
something greater than *Gone
to the mall, be back soon*.

3.

At a party years ago, the garrulous
stock broker, son of a cattleman, regaled us
with stories from down on the farm.
Cows, he explained, are the dumbest
creatures on earth, the only ones
that will shit in the same water they drink.
To which I, a little drunk, muttered: *Moo.*

4.

Even if the planters arrive tomorrow, horny
kids in ponytails and fleece, it will take a decade
for the fast-growing pines to rise above
the brambles and weed trees. What is ten years'
ugliness to a forest? The instant
it takes this blemish to disappear
under the plane's wing.

5.

In Peru, on a wide plain
near the town of Nazca, our ancestors
left the most remarkable signs, geoglyphs
stretching for miles, triangles, parallel lines
that predict the positions of stars and planets.
More ancient still, the biomorphs,
a 1,000-foot-long pelican, a hummingbird,
a snake, a spider. Giant figures
only discovered in the 1930s
when we began to colonize the air.
They weren't meant for us, but for a god
who lived in the sky. If any remain up there,
how will we be known to them, by what
broad strokes and sweeping statements,
what emblems of erasure?

6.

The hillside shaved with a dull blade,
a gap my mind worries over like a tongue.

Close encounter
(Whitefish Lake, Late September, 1997)

Clouds of mayflies and miller moths
drawn to one of the few lights left on
on the lake. I've put the paper down
to watch them glance off the window
over and over, skittering like electrons.
About to return to facts and arguments
when something else, something
extraordinary comes to the light.

Out of all proportion, head and jaws
like T-Rex, it wades
slowly through the swells of smaller insects,
something from a Japanese disaster
flick. The perils of radiation, microverse
encroaching on human scale.
And its pod-like body does seem to
shed its own brilliance – neon tube glowing
pale green as iceberg lettuce.

It dithers.
Like the Sunday driver who hesitates,
hesitates all the way to town.
This creature whose forewings most closely
resemble leaves and whose diet
consists of those very leaves.
                              'Ears'
on its front legs, rasps and ridges
at the base of the outer wings which when rubbed
like a fiddle and bow...
everything I recall
from the *Guide to Familiar Insects*.

Only there's nothing familiar about it.
I call you over and together we stare
as the giant inches across the glass.
                          The twin moons
of our faces crowding the pane. Then,
as suddenly as it appeared,
it lets go – relinquishing
itself to the darkness; cool autumn
air.

How to be here. And how to leave.

Ötzi

1.

After dark millennia, the roof groaning
above you, ice beating a slow retreat,
your body comes back to light, thaws
during the day, freezes again at night.

Then your rude awakening –
jackhammer drilling a hole in your hip,
thigh rent to the bone, penis severed
by the blade of a shovel. Unable to conceive

of your provenance, they mistake you
for a music teacher who took a hike in 1941.
While you lie in the morgue, waiting
for a positive ID, fungus creeps over your skin.

2.

I do not think I will visit Bolzano
where you are on public display
in a refrigerated cell, illumined
by greenish light that burns cold.

I won't stand in line to peer
through the porthole and behold
you with that mixture of
familiarity and estrangement
we reserve for monkeys at the zoo.

Pried from a 5,000-year dream,
a door to the sun flung open,
only to have distant relatives
seize your assets, squabble
over ownership. Forgive us

our scalpels and syringes –
exploring a toad's insides
with the dull point of a pocket-knife –
as we forgive your silences. Children
who never knew our fathers, we are

greedy for origin. What have we learned?
Your brain was not so large as ours.
You had high cholesterol, tattoos
to ease the pain of arthritis.
Blue eyes. Regular haircuts.

Kith and kin to you, black sheep,
I wish those hikers had never strayed
from the path, the clean Alpine air
had allowed your soft tissues to turn
into grave dust instead of leather.

I would be your pallbearer, escort you
back to the glacier and bury you deeply
and properly under the ice. For now –
which is not so long – I'll pay my respects
by not coming during visiting hours.

Whitefish Lake
(for Peter & Lorna Terburg)

1.

When things are no longer good enough
for the house on Ellerbeck, they must retire here:

chipped plates and aluminum pots, warped bottoms
rattling on the burner as water comes to a boil.

In the bedroom, a faded lithograph: two horned owls
knit their talons to a pine bough, their stare unnerving

at first, then a comfort – someone to watch over us.
The old concave mattress, a nest. We must sleep

practically on top of one another, mouth pressed
to your collarbone so no sound of our love-making

escapes the thin plywood walls. I sigh, close my eyes,
open them in time to jerk the wheel, the car drifting

over the unpaved shoulder. A long drive
after work on Friday night, leaving the city

in the mirrors, shawl of smog, traffic snarling
for a hundred kilometres in every direction.

The dog can't get comfortable in the back seat, keeps
getting up and turning around, getting up and turning

until it's you who barks: For god's sake, settle down!
We can't get there soon enough, worn out, sorely

in need of spiritual detox. The only place we know
where nothing changes: welcome

sign made of hooked yarn, yellow map smudged brown
where fingers have charted boat trips to Jones Falls,

Seeley's Bay. We turn off Hwy. 15 onto loose gravel.
The dog, smelling the lake and spruce woods,

scrambles between the seats, shoves his wet
snout into the air vent. You sputter, laughing

as tail wags spaniel, flurries of fur filling the car.

2.

Cottage life doesn't come naturally to them, the bookshelf
lined with dog-eared instruction manuals: *Small Gas Engines*,

101 Tips to Improve Your Fishing. Survivors of the war
in Holland, righteous gentiles who helped to hide Jews.

Peter at work in the shipyards – the man at the forge
tossing hot rivets into the air; twenty feet up on a scaffold,

the catcher with his tin dish, an offering to the young god
hammering them in to join the hull plates.

Lorna in charge of the mayor's household, then her own,
until forced to flee with two baby girls, eighty miles on foot,

Amsterdam to Staphorst, her body wracked with fever.
One of her daughter's earliest memories: a horse

running from a burning barn, its mane on fire. Forgive them
if they look ill-at-ease in Muskoka chairs. Lorna's resolve

to prepare a proper meal, hotdogs an insult to the palate.
Years with nothing to eat but pig food – boiled cabbage,

mealy turnips. She stands at the electric stove
while the cottage bakes in the sun, cicadas

droning in the maples; Peter disappears into his workshop
at the bottom of the hill, the bell tones of hammered iron.

In a week's time, he will present a weather vane,
a hummingbird's weightless hover flash-focused

in black metal. The alchemy of his hands.
He grips each of his grandchildren in a bearhug,

lifting them off their feet. If a cello could laugh,
it would sound like this: great guffaws rumbling up

from the well of his belly. Lorna's capacious heart
the only match for his own. Even as a girl, quietly

controlling, a matriarch in the making. Now this tiny woman
pinches the tendon behind your elbow until your eyes water:

Come dear, let me show you what needs to be done.

3.

Your last words: I'm going somewhere,
do you want to come with me?

I don't know where you've gone, Oma,
but I'd like to believe you linger here

in this place that you lived: the cabin
built high upon rock, a steep path down to water.

Invited by your daughter's daughter
to spend the weekend, I understood

I was standing in the vestibule
of the church of the forest.

Everywhere, there were signs, wonders.
The lake a mirror held up to clouds, woods

you could get lost in. And a pair of darning needles,
their prismatic wings, flickering.

Opa calling up the stairs: Wake up, girls, it's time
to enjoy Canada's great out-of-doors.

Out canoeing, we met a heron, curiously
cat-like, contemplating the murky green depths.

As we drew closer, the wizened head
swivelled on its stalk. Slowly, calmly

it unfolded its wings – garage doors opening
by remote control – and flew off over the trees, burden

and its lifting. Later, we watched the lake
turn to ink, a falling star slide down the slope of sky.

Oma, we miss you terribly; Opa most of all.
For 65 years, you never were apart. Still,

one could do worse than haunt these waters:
the silent V of a muskrat swimming to shore,

a flotilla of fireflies moored in the swamp, tiny lamps
strung upon the air, brief exhalations of light.

Red planet
(August 27, 2003)

Tonight we're on the front porch,
our closest neighbour paying us a visit

after 60,000 years. We won't get seats
as good as these again. Pennant of pale fire

hanging over Lake Ontario, so bright at first
we mistake it for a 747. Mars shines on us,

35 million miles away, a whisker
in astronomical terms. Approximately

the distance between a man and his emotions,
my wife observes. We've been arguing

for days, keeping at arm's length,
elliptical orbits that carry us far

from one another, set us hurtling
through the dark alone. I reach, pull my lover closer,

almost crushing her. We will ride out the night
in parallel, small boats laying-to in a gale.

We have short lives, shorter
attention spans. The origin of desire –

from the Latin *de-* [to cease] and *sidus* [star].
To stop fixating on the stars, eyes

bigger than our stomachs, and turn
instead to the earth, our own

heavenly bodies.

Rabbit ears (2)

The vintage TV set ensconced in the corner,
plugged in and powered up, we take turns

manipulating the silver wands, dowsing air
until a faint outline emerges and enunciates itself.

You can't deny the religious significance –
messages drawn from the sky. As soon as I let go,

the picture flickers and recedes into static.
Janet suggests it might help if we chanted spells.

I ground the antenna while she watches a sitcom.
In black and white, everything looks like history,

its pledge to authenticity. The brainchild of one
Marvin P. Middlemark whose other, more obscure

inventions include the water-powered potato peeler
and self-rejuvenating tennis ball machine.

Janet thinks you're supposed to adjust each ear
to the channel wavelength, high frequency oscillations.

My arm is getting tired. There's a Jays game tonight –
Who's on first? No, Who's on second, no…

Leave it here, tuning in background radiation,
residue from the beginning of the universe.

Our inheritance: ghostings, snow.

Basilica
(for George Amabile)

Of the cathedral that burned in '68,
all that remains is the façade, sacristy,

a few of the walls. I crossed the ice
to get here, walked on the Red River,

a clear day in March. Somewhere lie
the graves of Chief One Arrow and Louis Riel,

but I'm drawn to the lofty ruin, stone
framing a perfect circle of sky, cloudless,

preternaturally blue. A rose window sans
stained glass, portal open to the great beyond.

People have worshipped on this spot
for two centuries, their coming

makes this ground hallowed. The power
of religion, to give the infinite a frame. I believed

I'd outgrown my need for it, thought it like
those beds at the fur trading post, much too short

to lie in. I spent last night in my hotel room
with a book and a bottle of rye. Today, I find

I'm no less susceptible to wonder: flashing silver
in the sun, a jetliner enters the circle, ascendant

star in daylight, pointing god knows where.
The airplane intrudes on the commonplace

miracle of the morning, and amplifies it. Behold,
what we inherit, what we make.

Keith Jarrett: The Köln Concert

(Recorded Live at the Opera in Köln, Germany, January 24th, 1975)

Because in the coiled structure
of the inner ear, there is an oval window
and the notes pour through it
like sunlight through stained glass, because sunlight
in the far north
is a seasonal phenomenon – each year it arrives
unexpectedly
like a parcel from a distant relative;
at first, no one knows quite
what to do. Because the long
boreal night is all we can be sure of, because
we stopped praying ages ago – no
percentage in it – and yet
when we're frustrated or filled with despair,
we throw our hands up, look
skyward to that vacancy. Because sometimes
a single clear note, trembling *in vacuo*
is enough. Because the stars
vibrate like ringing bells, and their tones
tell us something of their interiors, how
they were born, when they'll die.
Because we never were
denied their music.

Finch Station

After a long day, you'd think we'd drag our feet.
But we're all elbows, jostling to catch the next bus home.

The boy and girl embracing near the stairs
aren't in any hurry. Their stillness makes them central.

He is tall and gangly. She, stretching upward
to meet his gaze, one of Modigliani's models,

impossibly long-necked and graceful. The crowd swirls
and eddies around them, the single-mindedness of water.

Neither is saying anything and I want to lie down
in their silence, shelter from the collision of voices,

sizzle of cellular transmission. Just then
the girl's hands scribe the air, flicker like chickadees

and he responds, finger-spelling the words
between them, the body's tones and inflections,

pursed lips, raised eyebrow. Something I remember
reading about Berryman, his secret hope

to be visited by physical disability – Milton's blindness,
Beethoven's loss of hearing. The fortunate affliction

that would rescue him from the machinery of living
day-to-day and bring him to his senses. If they could hear,

would the boy and girl still reach that other place
I yearn for? Looking into her eyes, the boy loses his balance.

They can hardly pay attention to what their hands are saying.

Notes on the poems

The epigraph to "Winter Songs" is from the song "Mon Pays" with words and music by Gilles Vigneault. The song can be found on Vigneault's album *Chemin faisant, cent et une chansons* (disque 3, Le Nordet GVNC-1017).

"Yankee gale, 1851" owes much to an account found in *Shipwrecks and Seafaring Tales of Prince Edward Island* by Julie V. Watson. Halifax: Nimbus, 2001. 60-71. "Lolly" is based on a short account from the same book (42-43). While the principal characters in the latter poem share the names of actual persons, they are fictitious inventions, as is Mr. Wier's letter.

"Come play on my island" takes its title from an advertising slogan used by the Tourism Industry Association of Prince Edward Island.

Many of the facts in "The lobster" were found in "Ask the Lobster Doc," a series of articles on lobster handling and behaviour by Diane Cowan. This column runs monthly in *Commercial Fisheries News* and is published online at: http://www.lobsters.org.

The first couplet of "Primer on the hereafter" paraphrases a line from David Seymour's poem "Thaw."

The lines by John Ashbery that introduce the book are taken from his collection *April Galleons*. New York: Penguin, 1988. 22.

The epigraph to the first section is from Eric Hill's chapbook *every tool is a weapon if you hold it right*. Fredericton: Icehouse Press, 1996.

The epigraph to section II is from Samuel Beckett's novel *Murphy*. New York: Grove Weidenfeld, 1957. 1. Several of the poems in this section including "Popular science," "With apologies to the Far East Fortune Cookie Company" and "Toronto life" originated from chance methods.

The epigraph to the last section comes from Donald Revell's collection *New Dark Ages*. Hanover and London: Wesleyan UP, 1990. 12-13.

"Ötzi" – AKA Similaun Man, AKA Homo Tyrolensis, AKA The Man from the Hauslabjoch – lived 5,300 years ago. His mummified remains were discovered in 1991 by two German hikers who had wandered off the trail in the Tyrolean Alps near the border between Austria and Italy.

Acknowledgements

Thanks to: Noelle Allen, Adrienne Barrett, Julie and Ian Dennison, Adam Dickinson, Shona Fizzell, Renée and Ian Gatrell, Eric Hill, Marg and Bob Hoops, Ken Howe, Maria Jacobs, Richard Lemm, David Seymour, John Smith, Matthew and Charmaine Tierney, and Andy Weaver.

Special thanks and much love to Janet, my beacon, my shelter in any weather. For all the words between us.